SCIENCE

OF

TIME

The Day When Self
Tells The Truth On Self

by
The Honorable Elijah Muhammad
(Messenger of Allah)

Published by
Secretarius MEMPS Publications
111 E Dunlap Ave, Ste 1-217
Phoenix, Arizona 85020-7802
Phone & Fax 602 466-7347
Email: secmemps@gmail.com
Web: www.memps.com

WWW.MEMPS.COM

The Science of Time

(Previously titled, "The Time and the Judgment"

Copyright 1993
Second printing 1997
Third printing 2006

ISBN10# 1-884855-93-8
EAN13# 978-1-884855-93-1

Printed In the United States of America

Table of Contents

Acknowledgement

We seek the assistance of Allah (God), Master Fard Muhammad, through the Supreme Example and Words of His Last and Greatest Messenger, the Honorable Elijah Muhammad. We can never thank them enough for the Supreme Wisdom which has been showered upon us, and as the Messenger himself stated, "He (Allah) give it me like a flowing spring or flowing fountain, the fountain have enough drink in it to give everyone drink that comes to drink. YOU DON'T NEED A NEW FOUNTAIN, JUST TRY AND DRINK UP WHAT THIS FOUNTAIN HAS;" therefore, we avail ourselves of the water without hesitation, because we never get full.

I would like to also thank Rose Hakim, Azzam Waathiq Basit, Dur-re Shahwar Aqeela bint Hakim, Taqqee Aamil Hakim, Junaid Shafeeq Hakim and Khalfani Hassan Hakim, who comprise the Secretarius staff. Thank you all once again for another job well done and I pray you all benefit from your labor.

Nasir Makr Hakim,
Minister of Elijah Muhammad, Messenger of Allah

Introduction

As this world turns, everyday the words of the Honorable
Elijah Muhammad, Messenger of Allah, becomes clearer
and clearer. I am reminded of a statement the Messenger
said; wherein he said, "We must become aware of the
knowledge of self and the time in which we are living. You
must know these things whether you agree that Elijah
Muhammad is on time or out of time. If what I say is out of
season, it goes for nothing. If I am on time or in season, then
all I say will bear fruit." This is the time when there will be
no judge sitting in a court, per say, judging you or I. No.
We will be judged by our own actions and the consequences
of which will be used to determine who we are - righteous or
unrighteous. Our ownselves will tell the truth on our
ownselves.

This is the Time and the Judgement of everybody and no
burden bearer can bear the burden of another.

THE TIME OF THE JUDGEMENT IS NOW

Greetings to you, I am Elijah Muhammad. The preacher of Freedom, Justice, and Equality to you, my poor black people who have been lost in the wilderness of North America for the last 400 or more years. You my dear beloved brothers and sisters who are [reading] to my [words] in this [book], I would like you pay good attention to it, our subject is the judgment.

Judgment has been taught and we have been warned that it is a day coming that we all will be judged, and whosoever Allah has mercy upon, that person have a great reward bestowed upon him. Because we live in a world guided by the open enemy the devil himself; therefore, being lost from our own people wherein there was no one to teach us, no one to help us, all teachers was prevented from teaching us, how very pitiful condition our fathers fell in when captured by our enemies, the open devil, in our native land through deceit, here we are today on trial before the God, who will judge us all.

Who will this God be? The Son of Man, both Bible and Holy Qur'an declares. He will be a man, a Son from a man. Son of Man. Not a formless spirit that the scientist and scholars of religion have given this name to that judge on that day, the day of judgment in which we now live, will be a man, for only a man can judge rightfully between man and man, because their nature is alike. Anything other than a man cannot judge our affairs. Nor guide us in the right way that we will be successful. It's got to be a man.

They ask, "when is the day of resurrection?" This is the day of resurrection, you're living in it. When is the doom coming? When will be its taking place? Don't hurry for that day, because you are living in it now. The days of the judgment of God upon the wicked and the correction in separating the righteous from the wicked according to many of the scholars on this subject would be something like near 20 years that time would be between 1380 and 1400 of the Arab calendar, and of their scientist which knows more about scripture than the Christian could ever think of.

We now are living near these days, the dreadful days of judgment, the end of the judgment, the end of those years now approaches us. We cannot say to you that which we do not know, less time will prove us liars. God have said to me that the time has long past due for the execution of the wicked the enemies who have mislead the whole world of black man except about 10% of them, so he taught me night and day in person for three whole long years, and about four or five months. And He still guides me, He still speaks to me whenever he please, right directly the voice comes to my ears from His mouth like listen to a word from you, whenever He pleases. He have taught me so many signs and so many ways that He can guide me, not by word alone, and not by seeing Him in person, but just by hints and I have learned those hints of various things.

2

THE SCIENCE OF TIME

The Judgment is coming; NO, it's not coming, it's here. Why should we have a judgment, why should people be judged? It is because of an act of an evil one that did not love truth and righteousness and want to make a complete people who also did not or would not love truth and righteousness and justice. That they may mislead us in the way of righteousness, and this way of turning the whole nation of the earth, the aboriginal people, the black man into following them, believing in them in their falsehood. He would be able to carry down, at the day of resurrection, day of judgment, most everyone that did not have the knowledge of him, of them I should say, for they are a whole race of people. This people that I am referring to is none other that the white race. They have ruled according to their god, Yakub who give them the knowledge who made them, and taught them how to rule us for the past 6,000 years. This has been done and they brought us up without the knowledge of ourself making us a prey of them in the day of judgment in which we now live.

Who will judge? The Son of Man. Who is this Son of Man You May question? He is a man that the Almighty God of the Black man's Nation made for the purpose of being the judge today. He's called and is known as the Son of Man. This makes is clear to you from both scripture books, that is the Bible and Qur'an, that you don't expect anything but a man to sit and judge over the nations of the earth on the day of judgment. As the **28th verse of chapter 45 of the Holy Qur'an, it reads something like this: " And thou will see every nation kneeling down, every nation will be called to its record." Now the 29th verse says: " This is our**

3

record that speaks against you with truth, surely we wrote what you did." This is the voice of the Son of Man in the judgment, watched over us and every action that we'd taken was written whether it was good or bad.

The evil opponent, the devil in person, an open enemy of ours, deceiving us all these centuries since thousands of years, today puts on one of the greatest shows that ever was put on by a man to get us to go to hell with him-temptation. He knows the nature of us, <u>that man always have that nature to want to do</u>. This he laid hold on, up until this very minute. He's trying to use his woman, his sons and daughters to tempt the black man here in America and throughout the world of man. They're in Africa, Asia <u>trying to tempt the black man to accept their woman and their sons, take them, don't have to marry them, do what you please with them, just so long as you commit the act with them, this is all we want to do,</u> they don't love you today anymore today than they loved you a hundred or a thousand years ago.

<u>What the act is, is to bring you in disfavor and dislike to your God, your salvation and your people of your kind.</u> This is what's going on today. We know what he's trying to do, and you should know my foolish brother who is now being tempted by them. They don't want you for nothing but their doom to hell with them, because of what, because you have a good chance, a free chance to go to heaven, to see the hereafter, but they don't have it. They were not made to go to heaven, they was made for fuel for the fire of hell. <u>They are a people that come in a vacuum between our calendar</u>

4

history of 9,000 years to 15,000 years this people their maker, the God Yakub, a black original man, he told them to go and deceive all you can for six thousand years, and after 6,000 years your brother from the East will come and eat you up, meaning destroy them. You have this in the revelation where that the prophet there prophecies of this coming out of the East and that they laid hold on the dragon, the white race, and cast them into a burning lake of fire. The contents of North America is that lake.

The judgment, oh the judgment, that dreadful day it is here, it is not to come. Hundreds and thousands of signs have the prophet sent before this day. I do not have time and space here to go over signs, for you are in them now. You see and you read how everything was foretold that is happening today. You say you don't believe that this is the judgment, tell me Mr. or Miss or Ms. have you ever seen a time like this before? Have you ever seen the clouds the rain, the snow, the wind going look like out of the very law of the nature in which they were made, to send rain down from the cloud to the earth. This rain has become an evil thing now. To send wind to satisfy the poor man who is lying in the dust, cooling him off from the fiery heat. But this wind has become an evil wind. She's blowing, but is destroying the lives and the property of the people that's in its path. Have you ever heard, tell of such storms destroying the property and lives of human beings in America. A country that claims that it follows Jesus, a country that people claim that they are better than anybody else.
Oh what a day, I could repeat with that old scientist there in the Bible he says " Oh woe what a day the work of the day is

5

on the woe I bear him witness. A dreadful day, a day in which the anger of the lord is kindled against the wicked and against all that do wicked, and against the proud who thinks they are too proud, too wealthy, have to much to look forward to other than bowing to God. But both Bible and Holy Qur'an say everyone will bow before the Son of Man. Every human being on the planet earth must submit on this day that there is a God over him. We are not made or created without an aim or purpose, so says the Holy Qur'an and this is true. The very nature of us warns us against evil, especially the black man. The black man's nature makes him to tremble in fear at times when he knows that he is far off the path of righteousness, because that's his nature, he was born, he was created righteous and has been mislead and pulled off the path, the right path. Therefore, now on opening his eyes by the powerful part of the universe, who came in the Person of Master Fard Muhammad, to whom praises is due. Who has taught me all that I know, who protects me going out and coming in, Who has promised me a place near him on the final end. Should I not be happy most anxious to teach you and preach to you of the woes and the destruction in which He have made known to me that He will do in this day and time.

We are living in it. Woe to America she's in trouble. She is in trouble. She has angered the God of Gods, Almighty Allah. He intends to bring her to her knees. He has the power to do it. Many nations before you thought that they was able to stand and contend with God and fight him with his own weapons according to the Holy Qur'an. He destroyed them, buried them under the sand of Arabia,

Egypt, Africa and other eastern lands, until today you will have to go and dig, dig, and dig to find the marks of their civilization. They're there according to the Holy Qur'an and according to our own scientist today who have went and dug, and dug, dug up the earth and made it clear that they found buildings down under the sands, brought them to light, some of them is unearthing themselves.

The wicked white race has been continuously to do evil and lead the black man into filth and evil. They are today, while they are in judgment, they are trying their utmost night and day, every hour twenty four hours, to get you to yield to evil and filth. Some of them here and there is against it and now speaking out against the evil doings of themselves, but they are absolutely made of evil they are not people that have some good in them and evil has dominated. No, they were not made with good as Jesus tells and teaches you and me and John the 8: 44. They was created a liar and a murderer, the lie could only stand so long as the light of truth did not make its appearance. But in this dreadful day there can be no judgment unless truth is told.

How well did the Jesus describe this day and time. In his parable of a Sower who went out and sowed his field with good seeds, but while he slept at night an evil enemy came and sowed tares among his wheat. Next morning, the day of judgment, the nearing of judgment, the discovery of what the enemy has done to the people, sown in their hearts of the righteous, evil and now they are practicing evil and must be judged according to their works. A dreadful day.

Four great judgment is now working on America, storms, wind, rain, hail, snow. How much of this is yet to come? Until that you are totally helpless. Pile snow up on your country from the north as your Bible teaches you in Job. He has saved this snow and ice, for the day of battle and war, It's going on their is plenty snow in the north, plenty ice in the north to be hurled down on poor America, who has no defense against such calamity. At the same time in the tropical regions, rising up in brewing storms in the carib area, some say caribbean, moving them northward and now westward to strike the shores of America, destroy her home, destroy the lives of her cattle, destroy her people. They're moving in America right now while I'm talking.

Oh Woe to America, Woe to America, she will not heed to the voice of righteousness, not even from her own people. There are some of them who wishes to go right, they're out there trying to condemn those among them who refuses to listen to the truth. These white people God will give them some mercy and will delay their time, their doom to some future years yet to come. But here is that man with nine against one that want to carry out the evil against the righteous.

When will that day come they keep asking, maybe you don't have to ask that question, when the judgment will come, it's already here just go to looking and see what's going on, and then stop and listen you will bear Elijah witness that we are in it now.

8

THE SCIENCE OF TIME

Great separation must take place I have been pleading to you black brother and sisters on the last page of our paper the Muhammad speaks that we should be separated from a heartless enemy and given some place even if it was here to ourselves. He don't want you to go free for yourself. No. He want to beat and kill you; he wants to deceive you so that you can taste his doom with him yourself while you have a chance. God has forgiven us before ever that we was born. The symbolic vision of the dry bone of Ezekiel is none other than you, and this lesson teaches you that God did give them life and they did believe, they bowed to Him and believed. The Holy Qur'an and Bible both teaches that he will force us to believe since that we are His. We are the people of the righteous. But you have been so foolishly following after evil that now you have become lovers of evil and haters of good, like the enemy who is misleading you.

I say my friend since you are weak too, as the Holy Qur'an teaches us, the Muslims, if you see something that is going to tempt you, cast your eyes in another direction. How can you love a people and you marry them take them for husbands and wives, while they has killed your fathers and your people all the day long every since that they landed on the shore of this country. Why don't you think something like love and respect for yourself and your kind? If they had been treated by you like that they would not speak to you, only with fire and iron, steel; they would not speak to you, the only think that they want to do is to kill you for mistreating their parents, and still is chasing their sons and daughters over the land to destroy them. It is awful my friend, great day.

The judgment. He is so wise and powerful. He makes everything of the creation to bear him witness, that this is the day of judgment, and then makes you and me bear witness this is the day of judgment, and the judge is sitting Able, Wise, knows us, and writes down what we do and say. Sitting Judge over the nations of the earth, having the power over their thoughts, making them to now fight each other, turning them insane. You see it going on so that they cannot agree, breaking them up with confusion, read your Bible it's there prophesied.

The Great and Terrible day of God is come and as it is written in the revelation of John, in the last book in your Bible, "Who will be able to stand." I say my friend, there is none that can stand in this time that we now are in suffering the lashes of nature; all nature now has been turned against America to war against her, and destroy her in sight. Everything is armed for the destruction of America. Her wealth, her money, as the James teaches you around the fourth or fifth chapter, warns the rich man, "go and weep, for the miseries that is coming upon him. You have done injustice to the poor the so-called American Negro. You have laid his hire, his wages, you have put them up, buried them in mountains, sent them out of the country to another friend of yours, storing it up to pay off the enemies of yours when they come against you; they don't accept your pay today, they have wealth, they don't want yours. No way can you pay off your doom. It is set, bound to come to past.

Poor America, as one writer says "Woe to the land that is shadowed with planes." It is America full of planes, soaring the skies over her country, but woe unto her the day, the terrible day of the lord, she has lived sumptuously, so says the parable of Jesus in rich man dying. But her laborer, her poor old so-called Negro the black slave, he suffered for the lack of even good food, and good clothes, and a good shelter; let him live out of doors, burn their house down if they had a good one, to show you how much he hate you to even live in a good home. Poison and kill your cattle to keep you from feeding yourself so that you will be at his mercy. Should not God do something about a people like that. Slip around under the cover of darkness and set your house a fire. Should not a God of justice do something about this? This is the day of Judgement, she will be paid back for all that she has done against you and me. She will be paid back. But she don't believe she is going to be paid back. She wants you to think that this is something or these calamities will pass over one day, and that we will be ruling you again negroes. But this is the way of God in destroying a people according to both Bible and Holy Qur'an teachings of destruction of people in the past who disobeyed God, and disobeyed his messengers and seek to kill the messengers of God, and some did do so. They seek to disgrace them.

Woe to America. The Judgement is set and the chastising is going on. The signs that would come to her, prophesied by the prophets of old is now going on, there here before our eyes. Four great judgments did he tell me out of his mouth, God in person, Master Fard Muhammad to Whom Praise is due forever. That is rain, snow, hail, and earthquakes, listen for your earth quakes, they're going on, in America. listen at what the weather man tells you is going on, in other states, is now going on. Listen to your friends tell you over the phone and in their letters what they see the dreadful things happening. No way out, it has already come to you. The shaking of the earth, leveling of the cities is the last thing that will happen. And before these things come to past on America on large scales, Allah shakes loose all places, a little small shake just to warn. And then at a distance afar off, she reads what is going on there: trouble, cities is destroyed by earthquake, rain is wiping away others, storm. I say to you this is the judgment.

I wishes to teach you more about this judgment...to finish getting you over into the knowledge that this is the judgment and the time has arrived that you and me must take a stand on the side with our God Allah, and the people of ours the black nation, or we'll be destroyed with the white nation.

THE TIME OF JUDGEMENT

We have been found by our God and our Saviour, our Deliverer, Whom it was predicted by the prophets, that would come and search the earth and find us. When He has found us, He would restore us again to our own says, Ezekiel and the prophecy of Almighty God through His prophets and Jesus made many parables of our finding by Almighty God and being restored again to our own.

We are to be restored. We are to be given a place on this earth that we can call our own. God comes not to affirm slavery, nor to affirm our slave masters as being worthy of being the masters and rulers of the original nation, the black nation, but rather comes to separate us and our slave masters and to give to us a place far from this people in whom we have been brought up by. Nursed with falsehood, deceit and evil, we are to be separated from such people. They are to be destroyed.

To you, this subject is the Judgement. This is the best and only subject that we can teach at this time with truth, the Judgement. For this is the time that we are living in. The final judgment of God. According to the English language, the judgment means the act of judging and this act of judging mankind according to his works, and rewarding the

13

righteous according to their works and justifying the two sides, the righteous, and the evil and granting to them their rightful places, one to his doom and hell fire, the other to becoming the master in a government and kingdom of righteousness.

We were found here in 1931 by Almighty God in the Person of Master Fard Muhammad, to whom Praises is due forever, the Sole Master of the Day of Judgement. He Who shall judge. He Who is worthy to judge. He Who is wise in knowing the deeds of mankind. He Who knows everything secret or open in the universe, The Wise, The Mighty, The Doer of what He pleases. The Most Merciful, and The Most Forgiving of sins, of which this comes by Him, forgiving we who has followed this sinful man and have committed the same sin through ignorance of ourselves. The day of judgment.

How do you know Muhammad that this is the Day of Judgement? According to the teachings and the word of Almighty God to me from His own mouth, in the person of Master Fard Muhammad, to Whom Praise is due forever. And from the scriptures, verification of what He has said and taught to me, and from the prophets of old and their prediction and from the time and the signs that is written in the prophets prediction that would take place before the final day of the judgment of this world.

Lets see about this day that we're looking at and is in. When we should expect the judgment? According to the teachings of the Bible and Qur'an and the sayings of the prophets of

14

old, and that which was communicated to me from the mouth of God, in the Person of Master Fad Muhammad to whom praise is due forever.

This world of mankind began 6,600 years ago, it was completed in 600 years after the father of mankind began his making. He had a completely new man, and had endowed him with wisdom and with knowledge how to rule us until our nation produced one that was greater than the father of this world. This has now been accomplished. It began, I say according to the teachings of Almighty God, Allah, 6,600 years ago.

When was that time up according to the word of God to me? It was up in 1914. Then why was not the judgment at that time? Why did not God destroy the wicked in 1914 if that was the end of the world? According to the past history of judgment and destruction of people by Almighty God Allah, he never did destroy them on the exact day that He had promised to destroy them. He had always been a merciful God, and He was merciful to those people in those days. He granted them an extension of time so that the world historians, writers, scientist, scholars would not charge Him with not giving them a chance to repent if they wanted to. So he have given to this people a chance to repent for the last fifty (50) odd years now, to be most exact fifty-two years from 1914. This is a long time to give a man a chance to repent, or change his way of life.

I say this people have not changed their ways to good, but have changed it more to evil since 1914, than they were before 1914, as you and me can bear witness to this plain truth, that they are more wicked today than they was before 1914. And instead of trying to repent of their evils done in the past 6,000 years, and the past 400 years, they have increased their evil, and more haters of the truth and more vicious enemies of the Divine Supreme Being and his purpose and his people who believe in him. They have become great lovers of unrighteousness, and haters of righteousness, so much so that a righteous person cannot talk a righteous conversation with this people, they're impatient to listen to him. They have no joy in listening to righteousness, they are bent upon evil and evil doings.

Mankind, who is mankind? mankind is the caucasian race, often called white race. They are a made people so God has taught me and so the scripture verifies, that not created from the beginning of the creation of man, the original man, but came after him and a grafted man from the original man. These people are referred to as mankind, or an image and likeness of the man that they were grafted from. Like the mule they say likeness of the horse that he was grafted from, or like the fruit tree, namely lemon, orange and grapefruit, the grape fruit is a grafted fruit from the orange and lemon, it only looks like that which it was grafted from, but it's not the same fruit. So it is with the caucasian race, caucasian, says Allah to me means a person that is weak bone by nature and stale faced. Their look is stale looking.

I want you to get a good knowledge of what we are entering upon the judgment of mankind, not of original kind, but mankind, the original is not a kind of something else. The original man is not from another one, but he himself is his

16

own father and God. The original man is God and father of
self, self created, not from another one. Be glad you are
black, be glad that you are black. White wish they were
black today, for black is the only thing that shall come
through the judgment, the only thing that will live to see the
hereafter, it is the black man. He's the first and he's the last

Let us take another look at this subject, the judgment. We
have just said how this word mankind came about, now
second, when is the judgment day? We have summed it up
in the beginning here that it was begun some times between
6,600 years beyond 1914. The Bible says God was six days
in making a man and whatever was created. Here we have
the universe even is much mixed in. The Holy Qur'an says
that God created the heavens and the earth in six periods.
But in Genesis you have a man who was created while the
Holy Qur'an don't mention man being created in six periods.
But mentioned the heavens and the earth being created in six
periods of time. Now the Bible says in Genesis that God
created man on the last day, the sixth day man was created.
God Almighty taught me that six hundred years the father of
the caucasian race was in making the man that we call
caucasian or the white race. This man God Almighty taught
me, his father was Yakub and the father of this mankind race
of people, as Genesis calls the man, an image of the God and
likeness of his creator. That's right. But the characteristics
was different and the color different, the characteristic was
of evil. Yakub taught him evil. Yakub wanted to try the
original man under the rule of evil and he made a people by
nature evil to rule, try ruling the righteous under the rule of
evil. For the next 6,000 years, from the time that he had

17

perfected made man into evil. <u>There is no such thing as</u>
<u>good as the Jesus says, and is taught of them, no good was</u>
<u>put in them, they were made evil from the beginning,</u>
<u>murderer, lying, everything but good, deceit.</u>

The day of Judgement is to happen after that particular time
of six thousand years ruling the black man. <u>He's to be given</u>
<u>a extension of time in which he have had.</u> <u>That extension of</u>
<u>time runs something like fifty to sixty years.</u> <u>But not beyond</u>
<u>seventy years.</u> This is what we have today. But sixty years I
think or not before that time, but a final erasing of the race
from the earth must take place now within the next ten years.
The time has come, the day we may expect it at any time.
The Holy Qur'an gives us in the 14th century after
Muhammad, between the 80th and 1400 years of that time in
the 20th year of the 14, the last of the 1400 years. Pardon
me for blundering, it is to take place. According to the Arab
calendar we're living in now 1386, therefore we have only
14 more years to finish the prophecy of the end of this world
between 1380 and 1400. Most of the scholars bear witness
that this is the time. This is the factual year, and we all
expect it to take place.

Today as you see, there is no peace wanted from this
people, this race of people called white race or caucasian.
No original people from brown, yellow, red, black, make no
difference, none of them want any peace with the caucasian
race, and especially America who has destroyed the black
man's brother here and named him negroes. And put him in
their own names, and now trying to deceive the black man
throughout America that their [white man's] name is his real

18

name, why? because they know that by no means can the so-called Negro be taken from them as long as the Negro holds on to his name, that means holding on to being his servant or slave of his white slave master's children. You will hear them many times trying to make the black man here today think that his real names is their name. They certainly have made the black man a fool. There's no such thing as the black people of America should be called by white peoples' names; they are not white people. White man called them by his names when he actually owned them, when he was selling them from one plantation to another to his brothers for burden bearers. Everyone that bought our fathers, he was called by the name of the purchaser. Now today for a hundred years, we have been considered free, and that we can now or rather are free to go back into our own peoples names, and even to return to them and to return to our native lands if we so desire. Of course Almighty God Allah can give a home anywhere on the earth that he desires to give us one. This is also written that he would give us a place on the earth and a good place on this earth, the best of it. Praises due to Allah.

Now today we are here and face to face with the judgment or the doom of this people and so many of us has been doomed by the false teachings of this people that today truth is thrown under their feet they cast it down and trample upon it as Isaiah prophesied in the Bible they would do. They don't want the truth, they stop up their ears, shut their eyes to the truth as Isaiah prophesied they would do. what made them like this? It is the enemy that has deceived them, their slave masters.

The slave master knows that he will not see the hereafter. He knows that he has no place of eternity, but in hell, not in heaven. Teaches them a false religion, a religion based upon a belief in three gods instead of one. A religion that they concocted themselves after the death of one of God's righteous prophets and the last one to them, whom they chased and caused his death 2,000 years ago. Now today they hang up this sign of a half nude man, the corpse of a man, nude on a tree, a cross, tell the dead, ignorant man to look to him and live, representing death and murder, murder and death, for life and for good will, for salvation, for equality, and for justice.

It is a shame, a terrible shame, that the poor so-called American Negro is robbed so today that he even hate good, because he have not the knowledge of good, he hate himself, because he does not know himself. It is a shame and a terrible shame. Robbed so complete until he don't know himself nor anyone else, the worse robbery that could ever be accomplished or given to a man, to go and rob the poor man of the knowledge of himself, this is a terrible robbery, it can't be equal with no other robbery. All the wealth that a man could give that would not, by no means, deprive him of getting more wealth, but when you robbed him of the knowledge of self, you robbed him of wealth. You robbed him of the knowledge of how to get wealth. You robbed him of the knowledge of the value of wealth. This is the American so-called negro:

Robbed so complete today that they even after reading the history of how their fathers were brought here, put on the block and sailed off as animals, and have been lynched and burned to the stake for every century since he has been here. And today he is being beaten and killed, shot down on the streets and on the highways throughout the government of America without hinderance by his slave masters children. Yet there are some leaders so ignorant and so in love and fear of the white man that they preaches the doctrine of equal brotherhood. They want brotherhood with their enemy before ever they ask for brotherhood with their own kind. Old preachers, Christian, so-called Christian church preachers, black preachers, preaching such doctrine that we all are brothers, classifying himself and his followers with being the brother of the devil and the lovers and admires, worshipers of real devils, their slave masters, regardless to what evil their slave masters do to them, they fear to charge him with it, they fear to go from it, they fear to ask for a place other than the place that the slave master prepare for them: that's a place of torment, worry, grief, and sorrow. This is a shame such leadership should be stamped out of the American so-called Negro and forgotten about, for they certainly is leading themselves to hell, the doom of this race of people and those that follow them as it is written. Jesus says, "How can the blind lead the blind, they both fall in the ditch together."

Let's take another look at this subject. Who will be the judge of mankind. Let's read the 31st verse of the 25th chapter of Matthew "When the Son of Man shall come in His Glory and all the Holy Angels with Him, then shall he sit upon the throne of His Glory" think over this. "The Son of Man shall come, and before Him shall be gathered all nations, and He shall separate them one from another, as a shepherd divided his sheep from the goats." This is one of the things, descriptions I would say the descriptions here is so perfect when understood, that a better one could not replace this. He, here, takes the sheep as an example of the righteous. He use the goats for the mischief making evil people, the devil. A goat is something that is always making mischief, you can't trust them. A sheep is a animal that you can trust, very humble, very submissive to the shepherd, and is a clean animal, it won't eat everything, but a goat will eat anything. So it is with the wicked, they will eat anything.

I say, Jesus could not have drawn a better description on the two people. Put one on his right and on his left. Do not get the idea my people that this is going to be a man sitting up and people sitting to his right and left, this is not the way. This is the predicted evil and righteous people. But actually **God does not sit in the presence or in public to judge on that day. He makes man's own actions to testify against or for him. The evil characteristics of man, his characteristics shall bare witness against him that he's evil, that will be the judge, that will be the witness of God, make every man's evil consequences become manifest his evil doings and the consequence for that evil will be manifest. This is the judgment.**

As the Holy Qur'an teaches us in the 75th sura or chapter Under "The time of the Resurrection," it goes something like this: "What will make you understand this day, on that day, when the self accusing spirit," think over that, when self accuses self, this is what this meant there, and won't be able

22

to accuse others of what self has actually done, but is guilty of doing these things itself. There, on that day, shall God make man confess his own doings. Every man shall bear his own burden. Qur'an in another place says, "No burden barer shall bare the burden of another." Make every man to know his own short comings; you don't have to ask others what have I done. It is not that he can take someone to defend him on that day like in the local and regular courts of the lands and the supreme courts. On that day you have no defense, no one can defend you. You will be your own self accuser. No one has to tell us what he's done you will confess it. If you are righteous, then your righteousness shall appear, and God will reward it. Though the book says it and this is true: "He forgives whom He pleases, and chastises whom he please. This means that there will be none that is absolutely perfect or clear as the Qur'an teaches. If it had not been for the grace of your lord, not one of you would have been made clean. This is right. Not one of you would have seen the hereafter, but He was merciful to you, because that you was a member of the original people of the earth, the righteous, and you was not responsible for being mislead, as you had no one to teach you against the evil guide you have into their hands 400 years ago. You was not responsible for your coming here. You was not responsible for your following the evil people that you has followed, because you could not go home, you could not get a teacher from home, they would not let one cross the Atlantic or the Pacific, to teach you and me. They won't do it today. But since that the book says He comes without observation, and He chooses His First Born. I'm the First Born of God from

23

the mental dead so-called American Negroes. I say, that He has forgiven you and me for that sin, as it is written.

Now comes the judgment: Who will be the judge? The Son of Man. Who is the Son of Man? Do He know the deeds of mankind? Yes! From the very beginning. He knows their history from the very beginning to the end. He has a writing of all their doings throughout the whole six thousand years of their time. Yes. What is the charge laid against mankind by God Almighty that He has set a day of judging them and condemning them of not being worthy to rule the nations of the earth, of black mankind. The answer is deceit, deceiving the people, the original people. Lying, robbing, murdering, the original black people of the earth, and killing the prophets of Allah, that were sent to them to guide them into the right way. The beginning of deceiving the man. The original people of the earth, Genesis, 3rd chapter and the 13th verse. And the Revelation, 12th and 9th verse, 13th chapter and the 14th verse. These chapters of the Bible declares this people to have been guilty of deceiving the people of the earth, the original people. Teaching them lies against God Almighty, deceiving them, putting them on the wrong road. I say you and me have knowledge of the time that we have known them that this is true.

THE TIME AND WHAT MUST BE DONE

The time is a teachings or a discussion among the people of the wicked and even among the righteous, is a subject that is never wanted. It is a dreaded subject for the wicked to hear one discuss his time of doom. This stands true throughout the ages.

We take our subject here from the Holy Qur'an and Bible. The Time, chapter 103 of the Holy Qur'an and verse 2, "Surely man is in lost." Man is in lost, he don't prepare for anything like the time of his doom. The nearer the time of his doom comes, the more evil he becomes, the more trouble he makes, the more disbelief that he have in the time of his doom. So I think it is most appropriate for me to use this subject with you, since that you are living in the time and ending of the world that you and me has known.

The Time and ending of the wicked, the Caucasian world, the enemies of righteous, the murderers of prophets, the haters of truth, and lovers of other than truth, the great deceivers of the nations of the earth. The Time, The time of the ending, we also must know the time of the beginning. All praises is due to Allah, the Almighty God, the Best Knower, Who came in the Person of Master Fard Muhammad, to Whom praises is due forever. I can never do enough in return for the blessings of this Mighty One's

presence and teachings Who came in our midst and made
known to us that the end have arrived. Who made known to
us the beginning of time of this world.

This world is mentioned of, its beginning and end, in
Genesis and Exodus. The time that this world would rule the
righteous is mentioned in Exodus 35 and 2, and in
Deuteronomy 5: 13,14. Six days shall work be done, this is
speaking to the race that we call caucasian or the white race,
are the enemies of righteousness, are the great arch deceivers
of the people, the aboriginal people, that they shall work,
their work shall be done in six days; everyday mentioned
here is a thousand years, each one represents a thousand
years, so Almighty God Allah has taught me, but on the
seventh day, or on the seven thousandth year, there shall be
to you, think over this "An Holy, a Sabbath of rest to the
Lord, whosoever doeth work there in shall be put to death."

Let us remember this a Holy day, a day of rest for the Lord,
rest from your evil trouble making, and deceiving and
murdering the righteous throughout the earth, for their
righteous doings, which hinders you from the people
believing and following your evil and murderous ways. It
will be a Sabbath of rest to the Lord, and if you work in that
day or on that day you shall be put to death. You cannot do
your work of evil in the seventh thousand year after your six
thousand, for God and the righteous will kill you for
upsetting the peace out of a day that is not yours, in a time in
which you are not permitted to make trouble to deceive the
people anymore. That day, that one thousandth year,
sometimes referred to as the one thousand year millennium,

will be for God to work in, not for you. He will put you to death in that day, find you working troubling the peace of the righteous, as you has done for the last six days, six thousand years. And that you shall not have any maid servants or man servants, nor any ox or any burden barring beast working for you. No more shall thy have rule over the people. No more shall thy have rule over the fish of the sea or over the animals and beast of the earth, or the fouls of the air. Your rule will be ended on the sixth day. Six days thou shall work. And six days it shall be done. This is Exodus the 35:2.

Let's now take a look at Deuteronomy 5: 13,14th: "Six days thou shall labor, labor to turn people from righteousness to wickedness. And do all thy work." This is the limit, you must do all thy work in six thousand years, for the seventh thousandth year when it enter it belongs to Allah and his people, the nation of righteous. But the seventh day is the Sabbath of the Lord, repeating the same almost word for word of Exodus 35:2, "It is the Sabbath of the lord thy God" The Lord here represents the Master. He is the Master of you, not that He is the Lord of your ways and nature of life of evil, but Lord here represents the Master of you. Praise due to Allah.

As Jesus reminds the Jews of reminding him when he and his disciples shuck corn and ate the corn after they were hungry on what the Jews call the Sabbath day, but he remind them that it was not made for him, the Lord is the Master of the seventh day. He becomes the Master, or he becomes the God of the whole world and people on the seventh thousand year after your six thousand. <u>And he made it very clear to</u> <u>them that the Sabbath was not made for him but was made</u> <u>for you the Jews, the white race.</u> <u>It is a memorial, a memory</u> <u>thing to remember:</u> Bare in mind that after you have lived six days on this earth and has been making mischief dividing and scattering the righteous murdering them all over the planet, your time will end. And in the seventh thousand year they will murder you, and rid their earth of such evil people.

When did the time begin? It began six thousand, no hundred and fifty one years ago (6051), according to the teachings of Almighty God to me. The time of the caucasian race. Now how does the time and calendar figure into this six thousand, no hundred and fifty one years ago? Most all of the scientist, especially the religious scholars and scientist believe that their time was up, meaning the caucasian world, in 1914, they were right, 1914.

<u>Almighty God Allah said to me that to keep this world from</u> <u>knowing the end of a time when it will arrive, they set their</u> <u>calendar back sixty years to keep them from knowing when</u> <u>their doom would arrive.</u> And even if that setting back of the calendar of time sixty years, they still have confusion in knowing the actual time of their doom. For the Bible teaches and the Holy Qur'an, that He do what He pleases, <u>He</u> <u>don't have to execute on the exact day for fear you have been</u> <u>smart enough to believe that you know the exact day.</u> <u>He's</u> <u>Master of the time.</u> <u>The Bible says He would cut short his</u> <u>work into righteousness.</u> <u>This is a hint that it can go not to</u> <u>the end of that time, because He can cut it short, and do to</u> <u>the evil the Bible says, that will be spreading against the</u>

righteous by the wicked, He would bring his work to an end even before that time that he had intended that they should live. But I say as Almighty God has said to me, that the time is now, the doom approaches, the year that we are now living in marks the end and the destruction of the power of the wicked, this is known.

I am concerned with my own people, not with the people that is other than my own, it is my people. If God has set a date of judgment or doom for this people, I have nothing to do with that, but I do know that they have not treated me and my people not even 1/10% right, I do know that, and you that is listening also knows these things, the time.

Six thousand years you shall do all of your evil, but on the seven thousandth year you must cease from your work. If you continue or try to continue to work your evil in that one thousandth year, you shall be killed. This is very wonderful to know these things.

Most surely man is in lost. My people is also lost in the knowledge of time, this is why a Warner must be sent to them to wisen them up to the knowledge of the time that they are now living in. Surely they are people who are drunk off from the cares of this wicked world surely they are people who love and worship the very enemy of God and of the righteous. They love not themselves, but they love the enemy, they seek heaven and salvation from the enemy not from the God of righteousness, who's hands is spread out inviting them to come into his mercy. He said to me that He would set us in heaven at once if we would just submit to

Him. He once said if He could just get half of the worship and the belief that we're giving to Jesus of 2,000 years ago, we would enjoy heaven with Him.

As the Bible says in one place, that the bird know their nest, and the ox knows his masters crib, but our people here, the black American, who its referring to, don't know their master. Their salvation, the God of their salvation, the time. We don't have to preach to you and show to you the signs of the time, they have already come and gone, but now it is execution day, and you're in the way, the time of this world that we have known, it is great to know these things, the time. <u>Not that it is the time that the righteous shall be destroyed, only those that is ignorant to the time, ignorant to the knowledge of truth, as the Bible mentioned that some place here, that my people in these words are destroyed for the lack of knowledge.</u> With radio, tv's, and with swift transportation and with the press ever publishing what is said, and the radio putting it out in the air, you cannot claim this to be no excuse that you has been deprived of the knowledge of the truth.

Isaiah says in his prophecy of these times, truth has been forsaken, and is trotted underfoot in the streets, this is referring to the truth that is put in the press that we know, yes, that we know how it is now done, and we know that you have no excuse since that you are now looking at the execution of the world of evil going into action. You see this daily, the call for war, and men to go to war, as the Bible teaches you around in a little book there that they call Job, he speaks like this concerning this day: <u>"As the mornings</u>

30

spread up abroad yonder mountain," the morning here means the same day, the seventh day, the morning of the seven thousandth year. "A great people and a terrible people stood in battle array." The mountains, as the sun is seen upon the top of the mountains first in the mornings, the valleys get bit later, represents here the mountains of the government, the rulers, the scientist of the rulers of the wicked world, they see the signs as the coming of the Just One before the ignorant people see, they know the time it should come, so they see their doom, as the Bible says in the Revelation, that it was the time of the dead, and the nations was angry, and even God himself was angry, for it was time that the dead, the ignorant, the blind deaf and dumb people of the earth, the black nation and especially we here in North America, should be given justice, risen up and we should have justice done.

This is now in our face. We see armies all over the world. According to these statistics of America publication, that she have a million and a half lined up around the earth to fight what would be her enemies trying to approach her; she will have one million and half people to kill first. She have also the whole entire ocean, all of it is fortified, her great fleets carrying deadly shells and bombs to throw on her enemies. She commands the high seas.

The Nation of the righteous have nothing of the kind out there, but the God of the righteous have power over the seas, the God of the righteous have power over the air, the wind, over the clouds. The God of the righteous have power over the still earth. The God of the righteous have power over the stars above and around the earth, and the sun and the moon.

31

He need not the carnal weapons of the man that is now lost. He need no such thing as preparation of war against him. The very rain drops is also artillery munitions for Him, the hail, the snow is munitions for Him, arms for Him. The very air that we breathe is also arms for Him. The clouds, the earth is arms for Him. If He shake the earth for just a minute or two, where will we be? If He sends power to the surface and demand her to shake us off her back, where will we be rising from? This can be done at the twinkling of an eye. How can you defend yourself against a God like that? He saw you flying and running from Him and His power before you was born. He had his prophets to put it on the page of History: You may ascend before the clouds, you may ascend into the heavens, but yet my hand, His power He says, will bring you down to the sides of Hell. You may go and lay down on the bottom of the ocean, as you are doing with your submarines; He says, He will command a serpent to bite you. A serpent here you must remember don't mean actually a live reptile, though there may be such in the deep waters of the sea who could probably destroy your boats. But nevertheless, this serpent could be a human being that have also prepared the same type of boat, and maybe a much mightier boat that God have put into their heart to destroy you.

What must be done, since you my people, myself hear all of these things going on and see the trouble times begin to get more trouble, as it is prophesied by Jesus. It is a time of trouble that never was its like before this time and never will be the like anymore. We should be preparing to do something for self. What was given to the righteous of

32

Noah, and of Lot? They was warned to flee for refuge in Allah to save themselves from the judgment of water being drowned and from being destroyed by fire and earthquakes. These people, all that they had, all the way of their civilization was destroyed. They were people who carried on a civilization of wickedness; God destroyed their very libraries so that we would not get a hold of any of their way of civilization written in the books of those days. So He destroyed and burned their libraries; He flooded their libraries of the wicked in the day of Noah, washed away their books that they had for records of what they were doing. The same goes for this civilization, it was an example and a warning for us in this day and time.

The Bible also prophesies in the revelation of John that everything of this world, the wicked will repeat, burn up, there will be no such thing as taking away anything of the wicked work to practice on or to carry into His world; He's self independent and He don't need anyone from this world at all.

I say to you my dear beloved people, you're being warned; 35 long years I have been calling on you to believe and offering to you what Allah has offered to me: set you in heaven at once if you believe in Allah. Just what are you trying to do now? You are begging the same people that has destroyed you mentally and physically almost to now turn and be a friend of yours after 400 years proof of their way of mistreating you that they have no love in them for you and that they were created or made to be a enemy of yours and mine.

Now what must be done if we would like to show the world that we want to be an industrious people and not beggars, why not let us unite together and make an appeal to the government to allow us to live somewhere in this country before it is destroyed, to ourselves. And give us some aid for the next 20 or 25 years to help us to go for ourselves. This also probably would stay many of the evil days that is now approaching America. If the slave master turn and do good for his slave, do justice by his slave, put him out of his house in a house to himself and not try to deceive him and make false promises that he knows he is not going to fulfill with his slave. Give his slave a place to himself, provide him with a start as he have helped all his life for 400 years to build heaven for yourself; do something that could be classified as good for your slave, maybe God would have mercy on your soul and delay the time by a few years of execution. But you are so evil you don't want them out of your house. You want to hold them in your house so that you can evilly mistreat them.

You know that they are blind deaf and dumb and do not know what it's all about. And you will persecute me and others who try to teach them what it's all about and even will kill us for telling the truth. Destroy our temples with bullets, and with fire. How can you expect to escape hell? We have no weapons to fight you with, you know that, nevertheless you will do all that you can to destroy us whether we have any weapons or not. You care nothing for that. You are happy to have innocent people to destroy who have no way of trying to protect themselves. This has been your way of mistreating the poor so-called Negro all their lives in

THE SCIENCE OF TIME

America. You take his life when he has nothing to defend himself with as though they had a machine gun or a tank rolling into your city at you.

I say my beloved people, the time has come that we must fly for our own lives out of this world of evil and trouble that is now going on to destroy the righteous from the face of the earth. They actually hope that they will carry the original, the righteous people to their doom with them, this he deceives you with, with promises of much wealth with him and even offer to intermarry with you. A few years ago he would shoot you, he would lynch you, he would burn you, for talking about marrying his daughter, now he takes them and puts them off in your neighborhood, teaches them to try and tempt you to go with them to their doom.

I thank you. Let us fly to Allah seek refuge in Him from this evil world and its doom.

SEEKING THAT WHICH IS LOST

As in the United States of North America, the Saviour, Master Fard Muhammad, was predicted to come to save the Lost and Found people of their own kind, the Black people of the Earth, from the destruction of the world of evil. They are by rights and are justified by right to be separated from this people who has made merchandise out of them, and unite them again on to their own kind. They can't be united on to their own kind until they first accept their own kind, and number one, have the knowledge of self and their own kind. This is the only way that they can be united on to their own kind.

Now the judgment, the year of the visitation of God Almighty upon America, they are here, and are just as blind, deaf and dumb today, most of them to the knowledge that this is the year prophesied and predicted that God would visit this country and this people with judgments of many kinds until that she bear witness herself that Allah is God who came in the Person of Master Fard Muhammad to Whom praises is due forever and besides Him there is no God. And that Elijah Muhammad is His servant and His Apostle. This you will do whether you like it or not. Allah have the power to force you to do it. It is written that every knee shall bow, every tongue shall confess that He is God and besides Him there is no God, and there is no Saviour for

37

the so-called American Negro until he bows in submission to the will of Almighty God, Who came in the person of Master Fard Muhammad. The visitation of North America, the judgment of North America, the number one enemy God have on His list to destroy; I say to you whether you believe it or not this is it. Surely they hate the truth that does not benefit them. Surely they hate for you whom they have robbed of the knowledge of yourself to know today that God is here visiting the country as it is written of Him, <u>seeking to save that which was lost.</u>

<u>Not Israel my friends</u>, it almost makes me sick to see you so far off from the truth, not Israel but you so-called Negroes the Bible is referring to that is <u>the lost sheep in the house of Israel, in the nation of the caucasian people.</u> <u>Not in the nation, not in the race of that people as a member by blood and flesh of theirs, but a lost member of another people that has been captured and now being held as a prey in the house of Israel, in the nation or race of the white race.</u> They have captured you, they have bought you from your people 400 years ago for a price. This is why it is necessary for you to have a Saviour to come and redeem you, because you was sold for a price, but the truth will redeem you as it is written, the <u>truth alone will free you</u> now. But you are hindered and you worship those who hinder you from the knowledge of the truth.

You sacrifice to them, you are willing to listen to their own falsehood against the truth then to come to me, the truth bearer and salvation that God has brought to you and me. Get it here, as Isaiah teaches you, go get truth without price of gold or silver. You don't need to buy no more truth the

38

truth is free. He again says in another place that the truth has been forsaken and is trodden under foot. For thirty five years I have preached to you the truth; thirty five years I have warned you and warned you that this day was coming, the year. Let us not try and concentrate on a certain day, or the hour, but let us remember that we are living in the year, this is the year, 1966 prophesied by the prophets that God would visit America with judgments, not with the actual, literal fire this year unless the enemy provokes it, but visit this country with judgment as He visited Egypt with many judgments until it <u>brought Pharaoh to his knees in the Red Sea, and at last when he was swallowing water drowning, he opened his mouth and declared Allah was God in these words: Allah-u-Akbar, Allah--u-Akbar, and Allah remembered him for declaring and bearing witness that He was the greatest and not pharaoh and today his body is preserved in Egypt there now to show you the man who opposed God. Show you his body there in the museum somewhere in Egypt, there are holding his body. They have found his body, and it is his body. Don't say that they don't know, if they don't know who is it to know. There is no other to know.</u>

Today we are in America, and God has found us and He want to save and deliver you from the judgment in which He has declared through the mouth of His prophets. And the judgment in which He has declared He would do upon this country to me directly to my face, it is so true. It is much verified by the prophets and their predictions of the judgment to come that I can speak it boldly for here you have the proof. It is made manifest; you don't have to question or argue with anyone today about the time you are living in, it's made manifest to you my people. I taught you for thirty five years what God taught me in the Person of Master Fard Muhammad to Whom praises is due forever. But you'd rather listen to a lie than listen to the truth. But I say the day have arrived, the judgment is now and not to come, but you're in the judgment now.

All the things that is written of the scriptures is now being fulfilled and has already been fulfilled. It is you, yet dead because you fear to accept the truth as the Bible teaches you in the revelation, <u>those who worship the enemy, the devil and his mark, they went down with him in a lake of fire alive, not in some spook form, but alive</u>, cast into the lake, because they doubted the power of Almighty God Allah over the power of Satan. Therefore having a doubt that God was able to defend them against the enemies attacking war against God and His people, and even against them that now have tried to follow Him, He warned them, He warned them Himself, he's going insane trying to destroy the people, or the nations of the Earth and keep his deceit, his falsehood still in the minds and the hearts of the people that it is the truth. Not so, not so satan. You won't be able to put it over, not so satan, God is the Greatest. Allah is the Greatest in the person of Master Fard Muhammad. He is the Greatest, He is the Mightiest. Let your knees bend and bow to Him. Let your tongue confess that He is, for you won't be able to fight a battle and win against Him. He have power over everything. He have power of the atmosphere of the Earth, He have power over that which is out of the Earth. Over the open space where there is no air. The airless space. He have power over that space. Wherever you may go, He have

40

power to destroy you if He wants to, you have not the power that He have over nature, you don't have it. I say to you my people that is [reading] to this [book], teaching here wherever you are and in Chicago wherever you are, pay attention to this sermon today as it is the truth and fly for refuge for your life in the power and protection of Allah to Whom praises is due forever.

There is no safe place for you but in the refuge of Allah in the person of Master Fard Muhammad. You have been taught, it has been told to you, you have on the page that Elijah would be sent to you, a man by that name in this day and time to lead into the right path. To make again a contact and a friendly uniting with your nation that you was robbed and spoiled from for these many years, 400. That such man would be risen up to join you again together, and that without such work, you could not be able to see the hereafter or be justified that justice has been done to you. Think over these things my friends, they are all written before you. He must first come, He must restore you, this is what is meant, He must restore you.

Don't look for spook, flying angels without flesh and blood come and telling you anything. The only flying angel is a message that flies without human body. The only angel is human beings. No such thing as what you have taken to yourself and interpreted as being angels. It is your mistake that you don't understand and will not come to understand what is the truth.

41

Today it's your own rejection, it is your own mistake, not mine, I tread the path. I do that which you have in the book, search what I have been preaching, and you will find me having all fulfilled these things, I have brought you face to face with God and the devil, this you cannot deny. I have warned you for many years that you cannot see the hereafter without a name of God. Your book, the Bible teaches you that. For many years you have known it to be just that, and it is written here in the Bible, every one that is called by my name: 43:7 of Isaiah, for I have created him for My glory, I have found him, here I have made him. Very clear to you, again the fifth verse: "fear not, for I am with thee", meaning God Himself, "I will bring thy seed from the East, meaning people and gather thee, meaning people, from the West, here in America this is the West. I will say to the North, give up the northern part of America, and to the south part of America, keep not back, bring my Sons, my people from afar, and my Daughters from the end of the Earth. This is a far way, this is a long ways from Africa and Asia either way you take it, right in the center of the Earth, think over that. The Son of Man shall be in heart of the Earth, three days and three nights meaning three years. Remember that, this is the heart of the Earth between us, Asia and Africa, here it is, it's America. You should know the truth, and the truth Jesus said will free you, he prophesied. Bring forth the blind people that have eyes and the deaf that have ears, think over that. Let all the nation be gathered together. Is this going to cause an upset in the nation, that they will gather together to oppose this return of you and me to our own? Yes, it's going on now at this very hour, today, they are trying to oppose the

42

gathering of this people, you and your return to your own they are trying to oppose it.

This is the judgment day of America, the time when every one of us must begin turning to our own. This is written and you know these things. And that day and time as it is written in Jeremiah, every nation or every man shall go to his own, and every man shall turn to his own. We must go to our own. We cannot do that which God does not want us to do, by no means. He can stop us, this day and time He's working Himself. This is the day of His visitation. Let's take a look at who shall be the judge in this day. Matthew the 25th and 31st and 2, and 3 verses of the 26th chapter of Matthew, 25th chapter, it reads something like this: "When the Son of Man shall come in all His glory and all the Holy Angels with Him." Don't get the idea that this is talking about some spiritual thing without form, these are people. The Son of Man, when He shall come in His glory, come in the time that He should rule, come in the time when He will be given praise and credit for his taking over the power to rule the righteous people of the earth away from an unrighteous ruler. I want you to remember, I want you to understand, the Son of Man should remove the idea of you looking for spirits, spooks, because it says here, He is the Son of Man.

Jesus prophesied that the Son of Man will come, not a spook, not something that is other than man, there is no God no where other than man, get that old slavery misunderstanding out of your mind. I can't say that the white man made you like this, but he have absolutely put it before your eyes to study in such way that he know you would misunderstand it, and to preach misunderstandings to you himself. This makes a slave who have been made blind, deaf and dumb spiritually by the master, unable to see unless master make him to see that which he have added out and added in.

Let's take a look again at the Holy Angels with Him, with Holy people with Him, then shall He sit upon the throne of His glory. Not say somewhere in space as some of you believe, but like presidents and kings take their seat of authority in the capitals of their people. This one is so powerful that He don't have to sit down in no certain city, though He's in and out of all of them. But He don't have to sit down there to rule and get a cabinet of senators or witnesses or helpers, He already have everything within Himself. He takes no one for His helper, but a messenger or a prophet whom He has chosen, or an Apostle, these are the only two. He teaches no one else the secret of His wisdom or power, but a Messenger whom He has chosen according to both Bible and Qur'an. The Qur'an is explicit on this subject that He uses a Messenger and reveals to that Messenger what He wills or whatever purpose or aims or secret he have to give, He give it to that servant whom He have chosen. Others draw from him.

This is the best way of all I want you to look at it: "And before Him shall be gathered all nations." Having the power to force all nations to bow. "He shall separate them one from another as a shepherd divideth his sheep from the goats." The nations or races were separated in the beginning, but

44

who have went among them and upset their peace is the white race who want to rule, who went after ruling them and breaking their ties of brotherly love and friendship as far back as you have history of this people. They have been making mischief not only among themselves, but among every other people, and now they have learned that God has visited you and me to take you and I into the heaven of His salvation, and to unite our hearts. What [He] is doing now, trying, as the book teaches you, which is actually trying to deceive you against the truth and is going after you and me, burning, shooting down our self and our places of worship. He have no respect for religion, only he just preaches to catch us with his kind of religion. Like a man fishing, he uses a bait that he thinks the fish will bite. Knowing the Negro, because he made blind, deaf and dumb the Negro.

Today he's angry as the Bible says in the Revelation. You will find it that when it comes time for the King of righteous to take over, when it comes time for Him to rule who's right it is, the nations was angry, and he also was angry, thy wrath has come. For it was at the time of the dead that the dead should be judged according to justice and given rewards to those faithful prophets work of righteousness. And that the dead, blind, deaf and dumb spiritually, they're angry because truth has come to them, they're going insane in anger. The book teaches you that, it teaches me that and I know you read it, we all know, we all understand, but I say again 66', it is the judgment, the visitation of God in America. She must know her evil doings to her slave; she must be given her chastisement that never a nation received since they've been on the Earth for taking an innocent so-called Negro, beating him and killing him night and day for nothing, only it is just her nature to murder, created to murder.

God wants you my friend, God wants you to follow me. God wants you to unite with me. Fear not for God is in person among us today. We suffer brutality and murder from this people, but I say today, 1966, will certainly bring a showdown, worry not, but I say bow upon your knees and do the will of Almighty God Allah.

The Holy Qur'an in the 45th chapter says "before Him all the nations shall bow, headed and kneeling." You shall see all the nations kneeling down. He will bring them to the record in which they kept themselves of what they did, this is your book, this is my book. The Holy Qur'an says there in the 45th that speaks against you with justice, get up my friend and fly to Allah I will show you the way, come on let's unite, we'll get no place, but to hell, for not uniting. I thank you and may God open your eyes, ears and hearts.

WHAT THE SO-CALLED NEGROES SHOULD KNOW-THE TIME

The American So-called Negro has been lost from their own people, and their country for 400 long years serving a people who have no love for them, nor mercy for them, nor justice for them, a people that is total strangers whom they did not know and they have served this people well for the past 400 years. They have laid down their lives like sheep to wolves for this people. Their carcass has fallen all over America, the western hemisphere and also in foreign lands in Europe and Asia. They have shed their blood freely for the independence of the American white man, their slave. And now today, they are sold to his ideas, they are sold to his way of life, and sold to his country and to his people, and in their hearts they have now more love for their slave master, their open enemies than they have for themselves and their own flesh and blood of their nation.

Blind, deaf, and dumb they are called by the Bible. Blind, deaf and dumb that they are called by the Holy Qur'an. A foolish people they are called by the Bible. A foolish and ignorant people they are called by the Holy Qur'an. This people the Bible says has been robbed and spoiled, so says Isaiah in the Bible and throughout the Holy Qur'an, throughout the scriptures of the prophets we are mentioned as a people that must be brought into the knowledge of self. We are mentioned that we are so ignorant that were following and being led by our enemies and has been made to like it, killed all the day long by our enemies with no mercy whatsoever.

Now today Almighty God Allah, to Whom praise is due forever, has appeared among us as it is written and it is prophesied that He would do: that God would come in the last days and would seek that which was lost. The average so-called blind, deaf and dumb poor, ignorant people of my own have even taken it, as it's symbolically given in the Bible, almost to be even four legged sheep other than themselves.

Now, this is the people that the Bible and Qur'an refers to. The Bible makes so many beautiful pictures and parables of we the lost and found people of our kind, once we were lost now we are found. God Himself has came here and has opened the truth to us, and made Himself known and His purpose and aims, and that He, Himself has found us as it was written that He would do.

Today, the average American preacher, who's suppose to know the words of God and understand it, and suppose to be preaching it are now more blind, deaf and dumb than their followers of the real truth and understanding of the Bible. Scared to death of their slave master's children to speak even

THE SCIENCE OF TIME

the truth that they even know, scared to death that they will not open their mouths for that which is their own salvation, and that which will bring their followers into the seat of independence of self, independent, that they could be set in heaven overnight if the preacher was wide awake himself, if he himself understood. But no, he don't understand, even himself. Therefore he's leading his followers down a very steep hill with no way of stopping unless that he open his ears and listen to the truth. His own salvation.

Their mind and their heart is set upon the white man to be white. They want to be the children of white people. They want to remain with the white people; they love the white people. They love that their children love the white people. They are a foolish people; they are the most ignorant and the foolish and the frightened and the most dreadful leadership that I ever heard tell of in all the days of my life, it is the American so-called Negro preachers. He would not even look at you if he thought that the white man didn't like you. He wouldn't mention your name in his presence for nothing in the world only in the way of hate, scandal and disgrace. He hates his own people more than he hates rattlesnakes. If he thought that the white man would love him for hating and persecuting and delivering his people up to the white man.

America is falling mr. preacher, America is falling, I repeat, and you're falling with her. You don't want anything, you're a lazy, don't want to go for yourself nor will you preach to your people to go for yourself. You are very, very much the enemy of your own people more so than the white man; I said, more so than the white man, who has enslaved your father and now you're a subject slave, a home born slave, a willing slave. You're more an enemy to your people than he himself that even the devil himself cannot be a worse enemy to your people than you are yourself, because you blindly and will not open your eyes to see, leading your people to hell with the devil himself. You don't want anything, but the way of the white man. Disunited, you pay no attention to that and cares nothing about unity with your own black brother. You don't even want to call one another brother.

For the first time have you heard a voice ringing in your midst, we the Muslim, we refers to each other always, in the public and out of the public as Brothers. We don't call each other Mr., we call each other brothers. We don't call our women folks, Miss, and Mrs.; we call them Sisters. This makes us to feel closer to each other when we say that we are your Brothers, and I want to talk with you brother, remove that "Mr." between you and me and I will tell you that I can feel the spirit of love in my heart then for my Brother. But if that old spirit of "Mr." and you are probably no more my brother than the caucasian, the white people, or that you're not as much my brother as they, how can we ever unite, how can we ever do anything for self? How can we ever go for ourself, how can our children that grow up and in the knowledge of trying to do something for self.

America is full of hatred. America is full of all types of evil. America full of filth. America is full of devils, and this is causing her fall as it is written in the book in the 18th chapter of the Revelation: She's falling, why? Because she has become a hole of every foul and unclean spirit. He has become a place full of devils. And the so-called America Negro trying to out strip the devil, to make the devil to see him a more devil than actually the devil himself. Teaching the so-called American Negro that he is not a devil, but is absolutely a divine member of the divine family, born in the divine family of God, but went astray following after strangers and now today they are practicing evil after the enemy, though they are not enemies themselves, but practicing evil after the enemy. This don't help you any at all to preach to this, especially the clergy class and the intellectual class. I believe now the intellectual or the educated class will still go in ahead of the preachers. The preacher is one of the most proudest and one of the most ignorant sects of all the Negro leaders there is in America. He is the worst man to try and tell something. He thinks he knows everything when it comes to divine. You cannot even hail him and talk to him even running, he will out run you to keep from hearing what you have to say if it's something that master don't like that he's listening to. He is one of the most truest and the best servant, and the most confidential servants of the white man that ever lived on the planet Earth.

You cannot trust him, he will get you into trouble. He will stand and laugh at you being carried to your doom with the white man. They are the worst that we have among our people, it is the poor black clergy class, hates you for not believing and following them in the foot steps of our enemy. We have a clear knowledge of this people; God has given to us a clear knowledge. We know their birth; we know their beginning and ending; we know them, and we know there is no such thing as having a re-birth into righteousness. We know that they are not capable of doing righteousness. They are not capable of accepting righteousness, because by nature they are created an enemy of righteousness and absolutely will not bow that, nature teaches them against only in a way to deceive the righteous that they probably is righteous, but it's different in looks and color.

But this my dear black people of America, for 33 long years, Almighty God Allah has made me to understand this people. For 33 long years I have been teaching you the understanding of them. They are very nice in a way to even help me to teach you the truth, even of themselves and even of yourself. Actually God, if He comes any way soon, or late, you will receive the worst.

THE TIME AND THE RESURRECTION OF THE SO-CALLED NEGROES

All Praise is due to Allah, Who Came in the Person of Master Fard Muhammad to Whom praise is due forever, the Lord of the Worlds. The long awaited Jesus that was to come for the past 2,000 years, has been looked for and expecting Him to come; the All Wise, the Best Knower, God in Person, and the Seeker of that member of the Aboriginal people that has been lost, to restore it again to its own, to bring it into the knowledge of Almighty God Himself. And into the knowledge of self, and into the knowledge of the enemy of God, the devil. This is the time that you are now living in that we are going to talk on.

The time is the main thing that we must agree on. And this is more important than anything else is the time. Without our knowledge of the time, there is no agreement with anyone. The time is the essence of all things, time. Now we have a history of every reformer or prophet, apostle of God in the past. We have history of them and the writers of these histories has been pretty much accurate. Now we come into the time of the world that we are dealing with here. This world that we often hear people mention and the world that preachers preaching from the pull pit that will be destroyed, and God will destroy it and bring about a new world. I want you to know that the world that is preached that will be destroyed is the world that you are living in. It don't mean that the earth will be destroyed under your feet. It don't mean that something is going to be destroyed like the earth above your head or around you. This is not the understanding, but the time of the ending and the destruction of this world means the people of this world, the people who teaches and advocate evil doings and practices. This is what is meant that this world will be destroyed and end of evil will set when the evil one was made or created, rather, we should use "made."

When the evil one as we call devil, satan, and many other evil and unwanted names, it is the people that has ruled the world of man, what man? the black man. This is the people that we are referring to. The world made up of white people who have exercised dominate power over all, black, brown, yellow, red races or what ever you are, they have ruled us. And now their time is ending on their rule or has ended. Just a matter of time now that this world will be no more. As it is written, here in North America, it is very very important that the so-called Negro here should know the time of judgment of this world and especially here in North America, because this is the place that God has said, in the Person of Master Fard Muhammad to Whom Praise is due forever, that He would first destroy here due to the evil done to you and me, the Black man of America. God will destroy this place first, He says. But first, the scripture has to be fulfilled. You must come to the understanding of the time and you must know your place in such time. You must know that you must turn from what you has been doing and from what you have known into that which now is being offered to you. That what you have been brought up in cannot work today; you have no refuge whatsoever in the white man's civilization at all.

I don't care whether it's religion, I don't care, and <u>that is one of the main parts that God will not accept today, religion of what you have known called Christianity. Christianity is turned down by Almighty God. It is Islam that you must have today. Without Islam you cannot see the hereafter. The Holy Qur'an plainly teaches us that If we come upon the resurrection day with a religion other that Islam, Allah will not accept it.</u> He accepts only Islam. Islam is the true religion of Almighty God Allah, and His Prophets. The religion, its name is called in the Arab language, but the word means only entire submission to the will of God. So it's up to you and me to submit to God and be saved, protected from the evil that is coming upon this world. You say, "we don't know what time," no one knows what the time is especially when it comes to the destruction of a people or a world like this. None knows that particular day, but Almighty God Allah Himself. But we have been taught by God and His prophets the time that it should be taking place. As far as the year or years is concerned, this is taught by the prophets of old, but you have not been able to understand it.

Since Moses, this is referring to the time now, there has been 4,000 years since that great wonderful prophet was alive, it's been 4,000 years since then. And this people, this race of people began 2,000 before Moses, and they were under the teachings of their master or the God that created them, that god was Yakub. This has been thoroughly revealed and taught, the truth of the beginning of the white man's civilization; everything of this history has now been revealed of the past. This is nothing new. Only to you my people who have not even tried to learn the truth. You were to busy trying to make friends with the white slave master and his children, and you had not no time to learn the truth. But we have now arrived at a day that will make you tremble. It will make you all but go insane, we have arrived to that day.

Now, the time since Moses has been 4,000 years, you remember, and the time since Jesus has been 2,000 years, and the time since Muhammad has been now 13 hundred and about 85 years, some say 84, some say 86, but the truth it is I think fits around 13 hundred and 85 years according to history. And these times of prophets brings us into a knowledge of the very set time of ending of this world, the Caucasian world. And that 2,000 years before Moses also brings us with the 2,000 years of his time ahead of Jesus and Jesus' 2,000 years now expiring and giving a way all of them for the last Messenger, with the last and final truth from God to do His work of closing out all of the fulfilled scriptures of those who went before Him. I say to you that is listening of my people, the time of judgment is now here, coming upon the place of wherein that you worship and the place wherein that you will stay as long as you see white people live here according to actions today.

THE SCIENCE OF TIME

Let us take a look at what is going on according to the prophecy of the Bible that God would go and search for the people that was lost from their own. And according to Ezekiel He would place them again into their own people, and into their own land. And according to other prophecies such as Jesus upon the finding of the lost sheep, symbolically, that these blessings would be conferred upon that lost sheep, by taking the sheep back to his native land and people.

We are living in a time of total destruction, were living in the time of the entering into that final war that so much prophecy of that must be fought, it cannot be delayed, it must be fought and today it is now going on. We also are living in the time that the Bible prophesies and the Holy Qur'an prophecies of this people, the scientist of the white man, going, preparing to conquer the outer space. This I say is now going on. For the first time since that they been trying to get away from the earth and go to some other planet, this they can do, they are doing this. And now you and me have witnessed this people going to the moon, we saw it on the television screen that he casted an object on the moon. This, if we have been here our grandparents would have said it was impossible, well it was impossible in their day, but not today.

Now they have also given us pictures of Mars, a planet that have life on it, they have been peeping in the windows of Mars that life there looks near like us. Men growing seven and nine feet tall, from seven to nine feet tall, and living a thousand of our earth years. They might know a little something about us if they had telescopes and what not and was not never at peace like we are, we always want to get around the other man's house, they probably would have known quite a bit about us. But these people are not as intelligent as we are. We are the most intelligent beings in the Universe. But I will say this the white man cannot live on the moon nor live on Mars, and this he will soon find out if he want to be fool enough to try and take a chance on it, but still this is true. If he carries everything to live on the Moon with him, he will have to keep himself supplied with the same, to stay there on the Moon with what he gets from the earth and not nothing from the Moon. There's nothing there he can live off of. If he goes to Mars he can't live there, because that environment is for the people of Mars who were born in it, like we're born in the heavy atmosphere of the earth, and this we cannot get out of and live elsewhere. We will have to have the same oxygen, hydrogen that we are using here for our bodies, elsewhere regardless to what planet we are on.

We also have to remember again, that old piece of our planet, as God Almighty has taught me, has been there 66 trillion years. She's just about worn out, though she can be revived, but she probably could contain many deep feet of dust almost ash like, if you notice when that the object was dropped on the Moon from the earth here, we saw through the camera eye on T.V., a great bellow of dust had risen from that instrument that fell on the Moon surface. It can be reserved and she can be restored, I'm not saying that she cannot be restored, she can become like she once was. That is well known to by the wisdom of Allah, how it can be

58

done. But I say the scripture has to be fulfilled, those prophets, you can't make them out of liars; they preach to us, prophesied to us the word of Almighty God as revealed to them in those times.

Now we see the Acts and doings of the white man, his scientists to day, fulfilling everything that the Bible and Qur'an teaches us and prophecy that will come to pass. Listen to this old Bible prophecy here that you has been hearing all the while, for a long time in Jeremiah here and other books: "Thou may climb up the heaven or ascend above the clouds, you in words there, I will bring you down into the sides of hell" This means that God would permit this god here, whom as Jesus referred to him as being the prince of the power of air. We see him as the champion now in space, in air. We see this fulfilled now. He is the prince of the power of air, he depends on the power of air now in moving across the universe from one place to another. This is true now. This is also true and perfect truth that the manifestation of God, and the manifestation of the enemy of God the devil, stands true that He did not come angry and added anything, but the truth to the enemy of Himself and of His people, this world the caucasian world, and that they are fulfilling everything that is written of them. But you my people the dead, mentally dead people, you must be risen, you must arise and take your place today on the earth as God Almighty and His prophets have predicted that you must do. God has put it through the mouth of His prophets and His work shall not fail; you must be resurrected, you must come into the knowledge of the truth. And seeing these plain scriptures being fulfilled by the people that have once held you in servitude slavery and now has not moved you out of the status of a free slave, you're still the property of theirs, who have not submitted to the will of Allah, who have not submitted to do the will of Allah, who has not listened to the word of Allah, Almighty God in Person, and Master Fard Muhammad to Whom Praise is due forever.

Here we have it written again in the Holy Qur'an that they will climb up to heaven, but the Holy Qur'an warns the white man that the heavens is a guarded canopy. It is a guarded heavens above us. Just how these guards are stationed or how they work, that is your guess maybe. It is known, and how they will attack this people, I don't know, but I do know that it is said that in one part of the Holy Qur'an that flames will be thrown at them, stars. We don't expect planets to strike them, but there's a lot of fragments that at a certain region that can be used to destroy them, as we call them meteors. When they hit the earth from the floating at the top of gravity, gravity brings these objects right on in. Now we have a region of stars that is close to our earth between what we call the outer planet and the inner planet. We look a many millions of stars here between us and neptune, platoon, these are outer planets of those stars, but they are absolutely a curtain like over us, or we say the canopy above our head. These stars, some of them are very small, can be used and if they are used and dashing them or having them to fall and strike the gravity of the earth they become flames. That is just what they will happen to come to. And there is no way for us to win against the creator. He has kept the secret of the powers of the universe to Himself and how he can use them, according to the Holy Qur'an, that He has made it a guarded canopy, meaning that there is power that can be used to strike out any enemy who would try to takeover and this is the warnings of the Holy Qur'an to this world, that if you try to get up there to use your power or the power of that region against God and His people, that you're just getting into a position to be easily destroyed.

There is no such thing as a way out after God get after you; you just have to submit, that's all you have to do, just submit. This is the time of the resurrection of the truth in the head and hearts of the so-called American Negro and I want to warn you that those who has put you to sleep are becoming angrier and angrier daily, because of what they see coming upon their world, they are becoming more angrier against the black man than ever before since they were put on the face of the earth.

THE TIME OF THE DEAD IS NOW

The time of the dead and what must be done: Since it is the time of the dead that they should be judged and should be given or be given reward unto the prophets. It is time. The resurrection of the dead brings about the closing out of a world. The resurrection of the dead brings about justice for the righteous that has lived in a world of unrighteousness under an unjust ruler for the past 6,000 years. Now what must be done at this time?

The dead must be given knowledge of the truth of God and of the truth of God, that they may be able to take a departure from falsehood into truth. What must be done for this dead man?

He must be washed and cleansed of the old world or the death of ignorance he has slept in for the past 6,000 years. Wake him up, put him on a new garment of righteousness. Put him on a clean garment. Give him a <u>clean heart, and a clean thought, thinking,</u> put him to think of clean and righteous things; for he was dead, and while he was dead, he thought over the unrighteous things and he committed the crime which the unrighteous committed; for he was dead to the knowledge of himself and to the knowledge of the true God of justice and truth. He was dead to the knowledge of those who deceived him. Now what must be done?

63

He must be dressed up into righteousness. He must be taught of righteousness. He must be taught how to distinguish between right and wrong. What must be done?

<u>He must be prepared</u> to meet his God. He must be prepared to now do for himself. He must be prepared to go for self and kind. He must be prepared now to build a world himself. He must be taught the way of wisdom and be guided by Supreme Wisdom of this world, a wisdom that is greater and is Supreme over what he has learned and what he went to sleep under and what he practiced under, and what he worship under while he was dead.

The time of the dead. The time of the original people that was brought into the Western Hemisphere 400 years ago by a stranger, by people that was not his own kind to be made merchandise of and to be destroyed of the knowledge of self, even those who brought him into a strange world. What must done?

He must be awaken. He's in a strange world. His eyes must come open, the spiritual eye. He must see the people as they really are; he must see himself as he really is; he must be awaken, spiritual awakening. No one has been able to awaken him for the past 400 years, 6000 years over the whole world of black mankind, pardon me I shouldn't say black mankind because he's not a kind, he is the original man and therefore he have no one to be a kind of, because he's the first and he's the last, therefore he can't be referred to as a kind. <u>So a slip of the tongue makes an error and a mistake in representing him as kind.</u> What must be done?

64

It is the time that the dead should be risen and be rewarded, they should be judged with justice. Justify them of what? They must be justified as being the members of the aboriginal people of the Earth, the Black Nation. He must be justified as being a member of God. He must be justified as being one that was in the creation of the earth with his God. His father is the original creator of the earth. He must know these things. By resurrecting him, teaching him the truth that he has not known, give him the truth, let him go free of falsehood, he must be judged and judged righteous. What must be done now with this man?

He must be returned in that in which he came from, his people, his God, his religion. He don't know his God. He don't know his religion. He don't know his own people. He don't have love for his God nor for the true religion of God, and he don't have love for himself nor his own people. What must be done?

Since he don't know himself now, since he don't want to come to the knowledge of himself, since he won't accept his own kind as his own kind, since he don't want to leave those who killed him of the knowledge of self, what must be done?

He must be whipped into submission, God must treat him as a father treats his disobedient sons and daughters. He must chastise them since they are absolutely so proud of being in the depth of ignorance and falsehood that he must be whipped out of it and brought into the knowledge of the truth, of the true God and of His just judgment. He must be whipped into submission because the God of truth, the God of justice is angry with those who has destroyed them and wishes to punish them according to their work of evil. But they can't be punished with carrying the dead along with them who are dead to the knowledge of justice and truth. They must come to the knowledge of justice and truth, therefore the God of justice Who judges with justice both the righteous and the wicked, He must bring them into the knowledge of Himself that He's present and He's angry with such world who has not ruled by the law of justice. They have destroyed the nations of the earth, has warred with the people of earth every since that they have authority to rule the people. They do not judge the nation according to justice; therefore God is angry; His Wrath has come.

The time of the dead. Angry, both the nations and God Himself. At the rise of the dead or at the time of the rise of the dead, the nations is angry. Why should the nations be angry at the rise of the dead, because that as long as the dead remain dead, they remain living and ruling the dead. But if the dead awakens and they being guilty of putting them to death, then they loose their power to rule the dead. This they see and they are angry. So the justice and the call of justice by the God of justice angers them in depriving them of their world to rule. But it is the time of the dead that they should be judged with justice.

We, the so-called Negroes, the lost and found members of our nation, God has come to judge us and to give to us justice in according to our place in the nation; justify us as being one of the members of the aboriginal people of the earth, one of the members of the originator of the earth, and that we should take to ourselves the power to rule our own self and our own kind. Take to the power to do for self as our fathers did for self before the creation of this world.

Time, the time of the dead. Time of the mentally dead so-called Negroes in North America, that they should come to the knowledge of truth and that they should stand upright for truth and justice. Time that they separate themselves from those who has destroyed them mentally. Time that they should understand that they should do something now for self. Time to begin a world or a government for themselves as other nations have done. For they have no more help from this world, for it is the time and ending of this world; therefore God, the God of justice and the judge of the world, both the wicked and the righteous, He will not permit their rule long, because the nation of righteous are to happy that they have come to the end of their time that they won't accept extensions of time for the world of evil and unrighteous, for they have been burdened with carrying a burden of unrighteousness, carrying the evil doers all of their lives.

For 6,000 years now, the time of the dead that they should be risen; they should come to the knowledge of the truth. Time that they should separate themselves from such evil world that they are now in. Go back to their own God, go back and join up, unite with their own people which has been put in many parables of the Bible that the Prodigal Son must be returned. He must go home. <u>The lost sheep must be found:</u> <u>the American so-called Negro is that lost sheep.</u> And be

<u>restored to its fold.</u> They must be stripped of the name of the wicked who they have followed and have now become one under their name; they are now being called by the names of the wicked which does not have any place with God at all. <u>For it is written, that the name of the wicked will be destroyed; they shall not live; the name shall not live. Their works shall not live. It is written in this book, the Bible. Destroy all of their works, burn it up along with the wicked and their name goes from the people and from the face of the earth,</u> for it was not the name of God, they did not go in the name of God. They went in the name of his creation, but not in the name of the Creator Who consist of one hundred names. Allah makes up that one hundredth. Ninety nine (99) attributes that make up His whole name Allah, which means He is The All in All, the God of righteous and truth, justice, love and mercy.

We must have one of these names of God. <u>The Bible teaches us that without the name of God we cannot see the hereafter. All other names goes for nothing and is classified as being the enemies of God's names, the enemy of God himself. The name does not mean anything of righteous, nor even wisdom, understanding nor anything in the way of justice.</u> A people called - think over it - fish, birds, bug, hogs, snakes, everything but a name of God, shows and testifies to the truth that they have not a good name. These names, the so-called American Negro is now being called and answering by.

Since he is now in the time that he should be risen from a mental death and be separated from those who has murdered and destroyed them, <u>he must not be answering to the names of the murder, to the wicked, to those who have robbed and spoiled them;</u> therefore the nation who has robbed and spoiled the black man is angry, and the God of justice and truth is angry with that nation or nations who has robbed and spoiled his people. He is angry. So the time that we are living in today is the time of the dead as you see, and as I see the works of Almighty God going on is to destroy this world and is to give justice unto those whom this world has destroyed, the American so-called Negroes. The time and what must be done.

We must return to our own. We must do for self. We must rebuild self. We must rebuild the earth and its people after the judgment of the wicked, the time of the dead is now.

NO JUSTICE FOR THE SO-CALLED NEGROES

If you studied the Bible and its prophecy concerning this century and findings of that lost member of the darker people of the earth, you will find that all of the teachings on this subject that you here and have heard coming from me for 33 years is none other than the truth. It is true that these teachings of the lost and found people of Islam that they would be found in the wilderness according to the symbolic teachings of the Bible of the earth, meaning a place of sin and where evil is practiced, and is dominate. Wickedness is dominate in the place and it is referred to as a place of wilderness meaning, lawlessness and savagery practiced there by the wicked.

America's symbolized or rather answers the description as we see how that law is ignored and how justice is not even practiced when it comes to the so-called Negro, that this must be the place where the finding of that lost and found people are in, and that they have been found and now something must be done about the separation and restoring this people back to their own people, and into their native land.

71

This teachings is so beneficial to the so-called American Negro than all of the history and teachings that he ever have learned since being in the western hemisphere. He has been found now by God Himself and the job and work of his restoring again to his own is in the hands of Almighty God Himself, which He will direct to the Messenger in which He chooses and makes of this people, and that Messenger has been made, and that Messenger has been delivering the message that the Almighty God, in the Person of Master Fard Muhammad, to whom praises is due, has been given.

Our subject is the time and what must be done. We refer not to the time of the solar system, but to the time of a people, as Noah referred to the time of the disobedient and weak people of his time, that was destroyed with the flood of water that was brought upon them by Almighty God Himself. And as Lot who taught and preached to his people of their doom before Almighty God Allah sent Angels there to destroy those cities of the places, as they are referred to: Sodom and Gomorrah and other small towns were incongruent. These places where these destructions took place is left as an example for this world, that she may know what might be in store for her or what is in store for her for her wickedness and savageness of the nation, her outlaw practices and injustice is absolutely disregarded, its disregarded and is not even in use in America when it comes to the Negro, or I should say the poor lost and found member of the Asiatic Nation, the black man. It's disregarded, there is no respect for a so-called American Negro when it comes to law. Even those who practice law that has gone through the training and teachings of law and order of America, they are not given any credit when it comes to trying to defend a member of their own race, the Black man.

I have sat in court time and again and again and watched how that the poor black lawyer is ignored by the judge, the jury, and the prosecuting Attorney, because that he is a member of the so-called American Negroes, who has been the slaves of their fathers and they have never given to them equal justice, and disrespect anything that he may use to try to get justice for his client who is black. This is going on daily in the court. Many of the American so-called Negroes turns to white lawyers to aid them in getting help in the way of justice against the white jurors because they know that their poor black lawyer may be an expert at law, but nevertheless he will not be given any respect whatsoever if the court does not like his crime. This has become clear as five fingers on black and whites hands that the poor American Negro does not have a possible chance when it comes to justice if his cause is for his own good and elevation of self and kind. And really he just as ignored as something that the law in America does not refer to. He has no constitutional rights that he can rely on. The constitutional right is for white America and not for the black man of America. And that as we learn and are still learning more and more as the time moves on. So the time and what must be done in this time, we must go after today to let you know what you may expect.

It is the time and ending of the American white people, number one as God has revealed. This is the people that is mentioned in Daniel's prophecy under the beast, the fourth beast being dreadful and more terrible that his fellow one and that fourth beast must be taken and must be destroyed and his body given to the burning flames. This is America so God has revealed. And truly America is the most strongest government of the white race, and the most vicious and cruellest when it comes to justice for the so-called American Negro. And that God now found us the so-called American Negroes, and He has taken it for Himself to deliver us by the hand of a Messenger, and that Messenger has already been sent, and is doing his work, and is progressing in his work by the help and guidance of Almighty God who is his backing.

This work is not say to try to bring about war and aggression upon America, but this work is to try to separate and bring out the so-called American Negro, the lost and found members of the black nation, from his cruel masters and unjust judges as it were in the day of Moses who's only work was to bring Israel out of bondage to the Egyptians. And that this people were destined to become a dominate race of people once they had been separated and their chains cut and the yolk of bondage removed from their shoulders of the Egyptians that they one day would rule, and this did happen. God desired that they have a place on this earth that they could call their own. He removed the original settlers of countries and gave it to Israel and made them a dominate people over the people of earth, and this same thing is now being offered to the American lost and found so-called Negroes. They must be separated from their old vicious [enemies, because God], He will destroy this people from the earth; their time is now up. And they are doing everything possible to remain except offering true justice

74

THE SCIENCE OF TIME

and freedom for the enslaved so-called American Negroes, the members of the black original nation of the earth. They refuse to do that, they refuse to teach him that he should go for himself and be united again to his own kind. But rather, they would like to continue to teach him to remain with him and suffer whatever cruel treatment that they still have in reserve for you and me. This is absolutely universally known, and the poor American so-called Negro should realize these facts and should unite together to make ready for an exodus out of their masters wicked enslavement and tricky hands to somewhere on this earth that they can call their own, <u>for there will never be any peace or anything like equality of the races as long as the inferior is here in America.</u>

<u>The American Negro is the inferior when it comes to the white man, because the white man owns the country, and the so-called American Negro owns nothing,</u> but in hopes of employment. This is his cry: "give me a job" which his cry should be "give me some land, and let me make my own job". But he has been so enslaved and brain washed by his slave master, <u>he even don't think that he can go for himself. He feels hopeless as Ezekiel prophesies them of saying such words, "that the hope is lost and they are cut off from their part," under the symbol of a dry bone or dry bone in a valley. This is true when clearly understood and interpreted in the right way.</u>

But I want to say to you: this time that now has arrived in America of the divine judgment against her, as eyes that failed to look cannot help but see that the divine hand of God

75

is working in America to bring her to a naught and against her on the outside of her border throughout the earth, God is working after America to bring her to her knees. He has within His power to do just this: to make the world know that He is God and besides Him there is no other God. He want to show the Negro, the so-called American Negro, I should say, that they have a God on their side. And that He have come forth as it is written of Him to deliver them, and to place them again into their own, and to destroy not only the powers of their enemies here, but anywhere in the world that opposes them by any nation if they opposes this little selected group of people. He intends and is fighting against them to bring them to a naught and working in the forces, I should say, using the forces of nature and even the minds and brains of nations against that enemy of His people.

I want you to be aware of this thing which is of truth that America is under divine judgment, and their is no such thing as a turning back and the scientist of this race see it and know it, but wishes to blind her poor slave to hold him in subjection to deprive him of the salvation in which God today desires to give to him. The true knowledge of God is now being taught to our people. The true knowledge of self is now being taught to them, but we have a wise and a very tricky enemy who wishes to deceive them and is working among them day and night to make them to believe that this is not the truth. <u>There are some few white people I will give credit that they are not all a hundred per cent alike, but you do not know how to distinguish them, you have not been taught how to distinguish those who are not a hundred per cent as the others, but I say if you get knowledge of yourself</u>

and of them you will recognize them, and it's very important that you recognize them and know, as they recognize and know us. Now again the time is here, an now what must be done?

We must prepare ourselves for a better world. We must learn that evil and the following and practicing after the evil white people is absolutely now rejected by the Divine Supreme Being, and that He now begins a kingdom of peace and righteousness and the doings of good, where this world have practiced the doings of evil. Now God intends to make a world, a world of righteousness, a world of justice and equality, a world of entire brotherhood, a world of absolute peace and security and contentment among the righteous. You are elected and chosen by Almighty God for the planting and build a foundation, I should say stones for that kingdom.

As you see an example here of us, we are referred to as Black Muslims, but we are not giving ourselves no such name ourself, how this name came in, I do believe, it's from the press, but not from us. We are the Lost and Found Nation of Islam. You will find it written in the Bible that He went forth to make for Himself a nation. He refers to us in the Bible in a certain place as a nation. And we are a nation. 22 or more million of us here absolutely lost and found people of the Black Nation are a nation. And we as I continue to teach you, has become a nation in a nation, and that we must prepare for our departure from this people. It is impossible for us to get along in peace with a people who are by nature is our enemy. It is impossible for us to hope for a future for our children practicing the way of this evil people. We should began teaching our children the way of truth, and the way of righteous that they may be accepted in the nation of righteous.

We are in the line of divine judgment and must be spread out of the earth. There are many misunderstandings of us. There are many false accusations made against us. We are falsely accused day and night, there is no real truth is wanted of us by the people, because that truth helps us, the true knowledge of us, it helps us throughout the world to be respected as the other people do now, created out of the ruins and spoils, people of ours that was ruined and spoiled by the white slave master. And that their children today desires to continue to keep us robbed and spoiled.

Integration with us, we must avoid such things as integration and intermarrying, courting and sweet-hearting with white people. We must refrain from such. We must not be tempted to accept them as our beloved wives and husband. This the so-called American Negro, must drop this foolish Idea. Even if the white man opens his door to you for such, you should reject it because this is a trap set for you today. It is not no love that they have for you, that they want to sweet heart with you is only to prevent you from becoming a great people. They don't like, actually, to see you clean up yourself so you will be respected. They like to see you in the mud so you won't be respected. And this is the idea and I warn you [to seek] your own God, your own religion Islam, and your own black people in whom you're a member of and stop trying to join on to that which is by nature not yours, and again which is an enemy to you and not a friend to you.

THE JUDGEMENT

I would like you [to] remember that the prophecy of the Bible if studied well - not to even think of the Qur'an, which we the Muslims use for our religious book and guide because of the purity of its text over the Bible, as it has not been changed according to the scientists and scholars on Islam - that there is prophecy throughout the Bible of a God coming at the end of the world and that God bringing the world the truth and choosing a down trotted people, or an ignorant enslaved people to be His people and revealing to them the truth of that which no other teacher have ever been able to hear or understand. It had been hidden according to the teachings of the Bible from the eyes and ears of the world ever since that the world had began. Now I don't want you to be surprised in hearing me say that this God has already appeared and is in person. If you understand your scripture, you will find that it teaches you of a God coming in the last day, and that we will see Him as He is and every eye will see Him, both the righteous and the wicked will see Him.

This I don't think you should make no mistake in understanding that the God's appearance in the last day will be in person, and not in what you have believed and what you have desired that He be in, some kind of spirit form. We cannot see spirits, and spirits cannot guide us in the way of human beings. They are not human beings themselves and so how can they have any interest in the affairs of a human being. The spirit so often misunderstood and misquoted or preached, means in many instances, the energy of a person, or the life of a person. It doesn't mean some individual spirit standing out here having the authority to tell us what to do and what we shouldn't do, because a spirit or energy always is produce by matter.

We cannot find spirit or energy unless we find the base of it, it has a base and that base is always something of real that we can see and understand, and therefore we cannot say that the God would come in such form or spirit when we gives that God a masculine name and a pronoun; the pronoun of He and Him or Thee God cannot refer to a spirit or spook, it refers to a human being or a being like a human being. It's got to be a being, because it have the pronoun of a human being. And therefore our own nature will not allow us to say or preach "thee spirit will come" or the spirit god, we always want to represent Him under the pronoun of he or him coming, in fact about it, if you are made in the image of God, you couldn't expect the god to be nothing but a human being. So on the judgment day or the end of the wicked world, He is prophesied as coming in human form so that we all can see Him with our eyes, as some blind teachers might want to persuade you that with the spirit eye, well then we won't see Him any better than we have been seeing Him for 6,000 years we have had dreams visions of Him coming and prophets and scientists have root of Him. But all of these dreams and visions we had of Him, He was in human form, and not something other than a human being, that is right, and we couldn't conceive of a God over a human family being other than a human being.

So this has blinded the world and the world today will dispute with the true God and true religion's teachings as something that is other than truth. But I say you had better go back and study what you preach, less you be condemn on what you preach or it will condemn you that we are preaching to you the truth and nothing but the truth.

All praises is due to Almighty God who has appeared among us, and this He appeared in the person of one Master Fard Muhammad, in the year of 1930, and remained among us as it is prophesied that He would do, around three and half years. It is predicted that He would do that, He would come and redeem or pay the price of redemption, and that price of redemption for the lost found members would be around three and a half years. And again it is prophesied in the new testament, <u>and some put it in the words of Jesus that He or rather there would be no sign given to this evil an adulteress generation but the sign of the sun or rather of Jonah. And that is this that as Jonah was in the belly of the whale for three days, so shall the Son of Man he says or writes will be in the heart of the earth for three days and three nights.</u> Now we must remember this kind of prophesy and get it understood before we start running off at our mouth over something that we have not knowledge of and if we have no knowledge of a teachings then we should not dispute with the teachers or the believers of that teachings. **<u>Wait until we have a thorough knowledge of what one believes in and then if we attack, we what were attacking and we know how to intelligently attack it with according to that which they have.</u>**

This is the thing we must know, and its always proper and wise for anyone who would like to learn a people to first learn what kind of a religion they have. This gives us a knowledge of the grade of intelligence that people have. If the religion is of the true God, then we know that that must be an intelligent people and we have to deal with them accordingly, but if they worship objects other than Almighty God, we don't have to much respect for them and we believe that we can always win against them because what they don't have the worship of the true God or knowledge of the true God and therefore that people will never have the help of the true God on their side. This is known the world over among scholars and scientist on religion, so therefore, an intelligent people or government first sends their ambassadors or rather, missionaries among people that they have no knowledge of their worship to first learn just what they worship, and in this way they can prepare best how to deal with them.

Now today where my people is so lost at it is that they believe that every thing refers to God or His angels, they all believe that it is something spirit or spiritual and that it's not real beings, its something that is the nature of spirits and there is no such thing like that. Even the Angels of God is not spirits regardless to what the scientists wrote or says today or what they contend that they be spirit, they're not spirits. When you get the real proper meanings of the Angels and the proper understanding, you will find that they are not spirits. They are human beings and is used as messengers, an Angel is a messenger delivering a message to a people or carrying God's message to wherever He's desiring it to go. Every prophet of God of the past and present are Angels themselves, and are not immaterial beings; they are material beings so remember this, and if you have any proof that they are other than that then we will talk with you later.

But in the teachings of the true religion for the last [few chapters], we must remember that we said many things. I said a true religion must come from a true God. A true religion is a duty that we must perform in the act of worshipping or paying homage to some God or some object that we hold as being greater than we. If we are worshipping the Divine Human Being, He demands from us entire submission to His Will, and that is the meaning of the word Islam. Islam means entire submission to the will of God. So therefore, now we cannot make a mistake in what Islam means. It means entire submission to the Will of God, and as I said in the past, that if any man or any religious believer, or even an infidel say he don't like Islam and will not believe in it, is one of the worst creatures on earth, because he declares openly that he will not submit to the Will of God and it is that person that God will destroy, who will not submit to His Will. Read your scripture for it. He is not bringing judgment on the righteous and those who will submit to His Will, the judgment comes upon those who willfully and knowing the Will of God, but will not do it who rejects submitting to the Will of God and subjects themselves to the will of the devil, and these are the people that the judgment is set for and the doom has been made for them in the beginning of their world. It is those who will willfully knowing God and His true religion of entire submission and will not submit to that true God or true worship of God.

Let us take a look at the emblem of true religion or that which we find displayed by the true worshippers of that God whether he be true God or whether he be false. Lets look a their emblems.

Let me first explain to you the emblem of our religion, Islam. We take for our emblem the Sun, Moon and Star as an emblem of our religion. What we actually mean by using the Sun, Moon And Star as our emblem, the red in the background of the Crescent represent the Sun. It means this: that as true as the universe, the Sun, which gives light to all of us whether we are righteous or unrighteous and that Sun vanishes physical darkness from us. When it appears, all darkness is vanished and that Sun shows us the objects that the darkness had covered last night, that we see them plainly today in the light of the Sun. Also that Sun gives warmth, heat to our earth and to our own being, and causes the plants and the seeds that is in the earth to germinate and spring forth and feeds it as the rain comes down from the clouds on these seeds and on the plant, and makes them or rather nurses them and cause them to grow in the light of the Sun, and by the help of its warmth. <u>This Sun is doing a physical work we call a freedom.</u> We don't have to pay for it. We never pay for the sunlight, even though there is many who may wish to sell it, as they have many artificial sun [and] heat [lamps] they claims today, so you buy that, but that's artificial. But Sun is free. Its light, its warmth, all of those great rays with billions of vitamins in it pours down on you and I daily, freely and makes it clear to us that last night's darkness was only false here and not real. The Sun is real, the light is real, so we use that to give to you a spiritual picture of Islam, our religion, our worship and the God and guide for us all.

The appearance of truth is like sunlight and it's represented to you and I as light in many places, because it lightens spiritually, blinded or darkened knowledge of problems or things that we did not know before the truth was told to us or before we come into the knowledge of it; so, it's compared with Sun and its light, so we use that. And as the rays of the Sun generates into us with all of its great millions and billions of vitamins into our body, it also causes up to enjoy good health. It strengthens us and makes us strong, so does truth, strengthens us and builds us up as strong defenders of that truth against falsehood and that truth vanishes falsehood and the spirit of truth within us which is the energy that we receive from believing the truth, that it is able within itself, to vanish and disappear falsehood; so, we must remember that. We have the Sun as a sign of the spiritual teachings and worship of Islam. So, the Moon, we have the Star and Moon in our emblem.

The star we use to represent this spiritual part of Islam's teaching. The Islamic religion is a religion of justice, a religion that justifies you and I to be good or evil, because of its truth and its worship; it justifies both, the righteous and unrighteous as being what they are. It makes us manifest as the light of Sun this morning made manifest to us the hidden objects that we could not see under the cover of darkness last night, so the Sun brings these out. So we are justified, we use the star as a sign of justice. <u>This star in the night justifies the Sun existing in the sky, that it is still there and by there little lights they are able to shine and guide us, especially the moving stars</u>. <u>The moving stars will guide us into the Sun light if we follow them, because they travel the same direction as the Sun, eastward, and so if we are lost in the night from the right course, if we take one of these movable stars which we call planets which is rotating around the Sun, it will bring us right back into the light of the Sun if we keep traveling eastward regardless to how dark it is or what part of the night we may take this journey, if we follow that moving star, it will carry us right back into the Sun light again.</u> <u>So we uses this as representing prophets who come and they are similar to the stars who, especially the moving stars, who always guides us into the light of the truth if we have lost the right path in traveling into that light or walking into that light.</u> <u>These prophets guides us right back in it and we find the light of God or we find the light of truth again and therefore we are happy and can walk without stumbling.</u> So this is why we have the Sun and Star as our emblem, and now comes the third which is the Moon.

The Moon also physically is doing a great work of equality to our earth, and it's also equal in a way of speaking, it is part of our earth, as God Almighty whose proper name is Allah, has taught me, and <u>was taken from the earth by one of our scientist some 66 trillion years ago and that before that time we used Mars as our Moon</u>. Now today we use what was made to reflect the light of the Sun on our earth. It also does a work of equality. <u>It helps the Sun keep the earth equally</u>

balanced, rotating in its kneeled orbit and also helps vegetation to continue to grow at night while the Sun light is absent, and also it has a great power upon our waters of the deep. And instead of our waters spreading out over us, drowning us over our land, the Moon keeps it reaching for it, turning up towards the Moon. And we say these are high tidal waves, called them waves, and we see them go up and they come down. This is the magnetic power in the Moon that causes them to reach up and that Moon is keeping them under control and they come here at the sea shore or the sand bar and there the go back again. The can't go over it, because of the work of keeping them in their place by the Moon. And also, there is much more that we can talk of the physical work of the Moon.

So it is in Islam. We teach equality, because we all are equal in Islam, the religion, the believers is all equal before God. We are not any big I's or little You's in Islam; we all are equal before God, as you have been taught that too. So we have this emblem as our sign of the spiritual teachings and workings of Islam. And therefore, someday soon, I hope to go over with it with you more deeper.

We take the sign or the emblem of the Christian religion. We have there a cross, and a crucified or a dead man's body hanging on it and this is their emblem that they say that they worship, carries it with them. And they worship that man who was killed among them and was rejected. This particular religion has a very, very ugly and a very gruesome sign or emblem. And they also say the same. They have a hymn that they use, that it says, "On yonder hill stands and

old roughed cross, the very emblem of suffering and shame."
We say so to. I don't think that a religion that they, any
person preaches that came from God, should carry such ugly
sign of a murdered man and then at that, they carry him half
nude, or rather whole nude, except just a little piece of
something to cover his shame. This is also ugly and
indecent to display a sign or emblem of a good religion of a
nude person. Sometimes they displayed the angels as being
half nude and all like this.

This is not good. So, my time is up with you and I must say
to you, may the peace and the blessings of Almighty God
Allah, Who Appeared in the Person of Master Fard
Muhammad, bless you to understand, and guide you in the
way of truth and righteousness, as I say unto you in the
beautiful Arab tongue, which means peace:

As-Salaam-Alaikum

As truth cannot be purchased, this book is a gift to you in exchange for your contribution which will be used to help us in building & remodeling our religious and educational centers. May God bless every contributor to this worthy cause.

Great Titles Are Available by
MESSENGER ELIJAH MUHAMMAD

Standard Titles:

- Message To The Blackman
- Our Saviour Has Arrived
- The Fall of America
- How To Eat To Live, Books 1 & 2

Archival Compilations:

- The Theology of Time *(Direct Transcribed Version)*
- The Theology of Time *(Subject Indexed Version)*
- The True History of Master Fard Muhammad
- The Black Stone *(The True History of Elijah Muhammad)*
- The Genesis Years *(Unpublished & Rare Writings of Elijah Muhammad)*
- Yakub: Father of Mankind
- The Secrets of Freemasonry *& many more Books...*

DVD & CD
Collection Also Available
Contact us through the information on the rear cover.

Printed in Great Britain
by Amazon

44081557R00056